MOODS, PHASES & FOOTSTEPS

PATTIE HARDING

BALBOA.
PRESS
A DIVISION OF HAY HOUSE

Balboa Press books may be ordered through booksellers or by contacting:

Balboa Press
A Division of Hay House
1663 Liberty Drive
Bloomington, IN 47403
www.balboapress.com
1 (877) 407-4847

Print information available on the last page.

ISBN: 978-1-9822-1995-6 (sc)
ISBN: 978-1-9822-1997-0 (hc)
ISBN: 978-1-9822-1996-3 (e)

Balboa Press rev. date: 01/17/2019

CONTENTS

SHORT STORIES

HELLO

Welcome to my world said the wasp to the bee,
I thought you could fly away and be free;
But instead you are captured by me.
Caught in my life goal of feeding my young
While trapped in my nest of misery and doubt,
Trying to comprehend what existence is all about.

These words are dedicated to the Harding Family. Read with love and smiles. See, I told you I can write ten minute poems and thoughts. The poem "Bright Tomorrow" was written to my oldest daughter, Sherlin with all my heart. "Unspoken" was given to my daughter, Yvette as an expression of love. Peace and love live within all who read these words.

My poems reflect different times of life and changing of moods that respond to friends, relatives, children, nature, and me. As you read my work, you are free to make your own footsteps.

Thank you.

Contact Me

Email: moodsphasesfootsteps@gmail.com

ASTUTE POEM

The Lord has created me even if I asked him not.

He allows me to progress through this world as my footsteps
are caressed by his rocky roads and my mind is soothed by
the magical tunes of the hollering, yelling and confusion.
He allows me to learn on my own as he guides me back to the
roads made of smooth paved righteousness when I go astray
even if I can't see his works or understand his words.
He gives me wisdom in learning even though I take
many chances in this ever changing world.
I guess I walk surrounded by faith that sometimes eludes my
comprehension of his presence with me. Sometimes I share with
others and maybe forgive my enemies but most times not.
The Lord, who created me, forgives me and in return he allows
me to live and search for my own meaning of life and death.
Still I wear a cloak of steel whereby makes me invisible from the
minds of fools and their wishes and prayers to save my soul.
I believe, but then I lose my acceptance as true.
I survive, but then I get tired of existing.
My light is fading as I grow, but then I still
waste my batteries searching,
For what my mind question, "cycles of life or just for fun"?

UNSPOKEN

How do I say I love you, with all my heart and soul?
How do I say I miss you, every day that I grow old?
How do I say I need you, and want you very much?
Day by day, hour by hour, I yearn for your tender touch.

How do I put into words, the emotions and thrills of the years?
The kisses, the touches and warmth we
shared and cherished so dear.

Why do I hesitate to say the words I hold so true?
I guess I'll just have to write them – MY HEART I LOVE YOU!!!!

BRIGHT TOMORROW

Into the daylight that shined on me,
Bright as the glow from the sun above,
I appreciate the Lord for this day, maybe,
Because of him giving me his unconditional love,

Into the glorious daylight as I walk,
Shadows are cast upon my soul.
Walking proudly into this day,
My mind is heavy as I stroll.

Ahead of me lies my soul's new birth,
That cast away my fears and tears,
Into my new beginning I shall take,
Nothing of the crisis from yesterday years.

The trials and tribulations of years gone,
The struggles and pain of my life,
Today the Lord has granted me peace,
And canceled out all of my strife.

ERUPTION

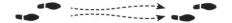

Out of the darkness that encompass the womb,
From a world that's dark as a man's tomb.
Into the light my soul descended,
Thanking the Lord for my humble beginning

Through the door of love and labor,
Into a world of many doubts,
I vindicate my presence with its label,
I, too, have cried and squirmed about.

Out into this world of suffering and pain,
I crossed the sea of night and day,
And yet I came without traces of shame,
As loving smiles encouraged my stay.

It's plain to see, this birth of mine,
Will changes the destiny of lovers in time.
Which makes one think whether it's love or hate,
That chooses the key to open a woman's womb's gate.

DEAR LORD

Help me to climb the ladder made of decision,
Help me to understand that your hands
guide each of our movements.
Help me to accept the consequences of my climbing and
to use each step, as it may, with wisdom and love.
Strengthen my body to withstand the load of my struggles and
aid my heart to carry the burdens of love and forgiveness.

Open my mind so that wisdom and knowledge
will not be a stranger to me,
Allow me to feel the wind from your breath, the
sun from your smiles, rain from your tears and
the love from your ever-forgiving heart.
Thank you kindly, Father, for I am but a poor babe in this
big spectrum of your creation, for allowing me to ask.
AMEN

I WILL MISS YOU, MY HEART

She sat by his bedside and looked into his face,
She smiled upon her older son with love, pride and grace.
She knew in her heart, this was the ending to his time,
However, her eyes embedded him deeper into her heart and mind.
"You're my oldest son" her thoughts conveyed,
And I have lived and watched you as you grew,
Bathe, changed and groomed you for this life you knew.
Now it's time to let you go home,
Although, I don't want you to leave me alone,
My heart is heavy as my mind ponders our events in life,
I love you, my son with all my loving might.
And I will miss you, my heart!!!!!!!!!!!
Mother

THE ERASER

There are holes written in my life contract, and
they have been scripted in it too long,
Now I want my life written and sealed without all these thorns.

We all are given a thorny rose to bear and clean by hand,
We are merely puppets controlled by God's ordained Man.

As I walk through life's valley of existing,
my way of life cannot emerge,
I need the eraser to come and help me to be purged.

My life contract lasts only a few years,
And in this paper is written many anxieties and tears.
A few days of begging and borrowing,
A lot of years of worries and doubt,
Times of wishing and hoping,
Many hours of trying hard to sort things out,
Closed heart and pondering mind,
One-way streets and dark caves,
Nothing to write home about,
Nothing valuable to save,
No assets or small fortunes,
Lots of wishes, hoping and prayers of all sorts,
Fake smiles and false well wishes,
Limited people to help me out.

I need the eraser to come and help me eliminate these lines.
And place in my life contract good deeds,
friendship, love and peace of mind.

FLASHBACK

I heard your name called, so I turned around,
I stood looking at you, as I wore a bold frown.
After years of pain, lies and grief,
You still looked the same, so that's a relief.

We should have never been together and pretending to be one,
But then I thought I loved you but now that seems plain dumb.

Boy, you took me through my life in a hot flash,
And I wasn't ready for that fifty-yard dash.

When we finally parted, I was left stunned,
Now my life improved and I know I won.
So hello and goodbye to you my friend,
The race stopped back yonder; therefore, that was the end!

STORM

Vociferous sounds coming from the sky,
One could compare it to one thousand jets passing by.
Whether or not God's talking or scolding,
The resonance leaves one's soul cowering.

I am alone in this storm

Lightning and thunder races through the clouds,
Houses, windows, doors tremble as the loudness vibes.
Trees, plants, grass, and debris dance as the strong winds go by,
Little children sit very still or cry.
I am alone in this storm.

Darkness, motionless embraces the streets,
Heavy rain bounces, prances and seep.
Thick raindrop sheets engulf the atmosphere
Dropping to the earth surroundings with
affectionate distinct caring.

I am alone in this storm.

All creatures trembling to the musical melody and many do pray,
Bowing their heads and bending their knees,
begging God for a safe and better day.

I am alone in this storm.

For me I just don't know here or why,
My body waits patiently afraid to cry.
Wondering what did I do wrong?
To be caught in such a twisted thorn,

I am alone in this storm.

AND HE SAT

He came and sat down by the water side,
And the water ran cold and the waves clashed against the tide.
The trees raced with the wind as their
leaves danced to an unheard beat,
And the clouds hovered above the heaven
and gathered into a massive heap.
And he sat.

The moon in the sky emitted a soft reflection glow,
Too soft to say it was time to come out and too
strong for its glimmer not to show.
And he sat.

The grass by the bank of the water appeared green,
And it wanted desperately to change its color to a softer sheen.
And he sat.

Even if I hope and pray,
No answer do I find today.
Faith is strange but some have it anyway,
Mine's here and gone the following day.

I wait, hope and trust only to find,
I've been left in the dust, only to whine.
Last to win but first to try,
I keep knocking myself silly but I don't know why.

I guess I just need to live like this until I die,
Too shame to beg, too proud to cry.
My life stinks.
As he still sat.

LIFE IS A CIRCLE

I wish,
      I can't think,
         I need faith.

Faith comes and goes
      I need patience.

I pray,
      I need words.
Peace, grace and mercy to us all!!

THINKING

I won't go,
But I must go.
I can't go,
But I will go,
I should go.
But can I really go?

Then I change my mind,
I will not go,
But I need too,
I should and I shouldn't,
But it's not that I couldn't,
I just got to make up my mind and stick to my decision.

FOG

It caresses the world with a tender kiss.
By moving here and there without a sound,
Passing gently over mountains, water, sky and the ground,
As it engulfs the surroundings in a loving embrace,
Moving peacefully and smoothly at its' own pace.
There is no secrets the fog do not know,
Its watery droplets touch every man or foe.
It curls, bent and moves in a wiggle motion,
It travels wherever it has a notion.

The fog teases the smoke from the chimney's stacks,
And laughs at the leaves that can't laugh back,
It mocks the exhaust from the cars on the roads,
And chases across grass as if it tickling its' toes.

It's a friend, a foe, a spy and a signs of new hope,
It's happy and carefree, and it never mopes.
It comes early in the morning or late at night,
Fog misty dew helps beautify Earth's heavenly light.

But when the sun rays come out to play,
And covers the sky, fog can't stay,
The heat from the sun dries its mist,
And send the fog home to wait its turn
Until the sun has completed its burn.
But you can be sure of this one thing,
The fog will be back and play with us again.

ANGRY

Why do I continue to talk to you?
When you make me scream, holler, and criticize what you do,
Why is it hard for you to see?
That your displays of stupidity sicken me,
When will you grow to understand?
I chose you to be my mature man.

To hold, caress, and protect me too,
To love me, understand me, and care about what I do.
But one day you are a caring soul,
And the next day you do nothing but scold.
This alter of moods can be confusing,
Your changing and twisting events make me not amused.

I will not keep on fighting things out,
I can change a lover without crying in doubt.
Therefore, take this warning as a method of stepping to the pace,
Or else your pseudo butt will be out of my face.

HATE

Sprung from the bowels of the pit of my soul,
Up to the vessels on a free ride call loathe,
One day was love but now there is hate,
Wishing you just tumble and drop dead at my gate.

At least I could mourn and cry for you,
Instead of wishing for some event to happen and erase you too,
One day I will hear that you are dead and gone,
And I will be happy and sing a song.

The asshole, jackass is now six feet under the dirt,
And I am still here to go out and flirt.

MISUNDERSTANDING

I snatched the worn, blackened chain from my neck, but then
I found that my hands were bound. I fought night and day,
to liberate the bonds that were preventing my freedom.
Each time I discovered to my dismay that when
my hands were free, my feet were
bound and vice versa.
The more I struggled, the harder I fell to the floor.
My mind played games with my body, and I played
along trying to forget that I was chained.
I needed my freedom, I could taste my freedom,
and I could sense my freedom.
I wanted to be my own boss, to fight my own
battles, to live my own life, to just be me.
There is no other like me, but then I wondered
"WHY WAS I CHAINED?"
My feet felt heavy in the ropes and my heart ached to be free.
My mind schemed and formed strategies.
Through all my troubles, I prayed, hoped, wished and
struggled endless hours to be free of the bond that held me

One day, I felt the ropes drop from my feet.
Now, I am free.
I can run, dance, jump, raise my hands, and open my
mind to allow ideas and thoughts into my inner soul.
Then the music stopped and the dance became tiring, the
knowledge boring and the going place a nuisance.
Now I ask myself, "IF I AM REALLY FREE,
WHY DO I FEEL SO ALONE?"

INUNDATED

Dear Lord in heaven I know not what to do,
Each day as it come and passes I'm asking you.
Even if you answering I am not hearing because of life's curves,
Even if you holler, I still can't understand your words.
I feel I am lost and forsaken for all time,
I wish I could have the answers as I pen these lines.
Confusion, worries and fretting about,
Just aren't helping me sort this problem out.
When you have time, dear father above,
Send down to me a special ray of your love.
Just let me enjoy life without any strings,
Then maybe all will be revealing about these problem things,
And allow me to keep and remember your intervention well,
Then I'll know what life's path I am to dwell.

FOR WHAT YOU HAVE CREATED

To gaze upon the earth and truly see what is being done to what you have created

To listen to the hopes, wishes, joy, sadness, happiness, sickness, and general problems of what is happening to what you have created.

To tolerate the lies, stealing, murders, rapes, robberies, plundering of each and all creation yet still forgive what is dominating their presence upon what you have created.

To smile with your sun's rays, cry with your rain and ponder with your winds what you have created.

To not allow the bitterness or hatred to take up space in your heart or mind regarding what you have created.

To walk each day with all, not few, not some, not many of what you have created.

To wake each and everything with your sun or rains and passionately put them to sleep at night with your moon glow what you have created.

To whisper, "don't worry, I am here and will always be here for you", to what you have created All your works and reassurance yet what you have created still desire more.

ONE MOMENT IN TIME

One moment in time, I spent with you,
Forever stamp in my mind, that we were true.
One moment in space,
We love passionately,
We left our cares, and embarked on as one.
No one can take that moment from me,
No one can dream how deep it felt.
Not a dream or wish,
That one hoped to come true.
One moment in time, I spent with you.
I can play it back, fast, slow or pause.
No matter how I think it,
It's there for me to enjoy.
It was very true, without the words I do,
That moment in time and you felt it too,
When we both let our guards down and loved true.

MY SILENT PRAYER

Oh, look at me Great Father.
Oh, look at me please.
I am flesh, I am human, and if you cut me I will bleed.
Just give me a chance, Great Father,
Give me a chance, please—
I've done wrong, I've done right,
I've fought pain with all my might.
I've cried and been lonely,
I've defended and been wrong.
I've trusted when I should have doubted,
I've loved when it was only hate,
I've struggled when I should have rest.
I've laughed when I should have screamed,
I've crawled because I could not walk,
I've been quiet and afraid to talk.

Oh, walk with me Great Father,
Walk with me and see,
See all the love and all the hate and all the anxiety.
Hold out your hand, Great Father,
Hold out your hand, please.
Take all your children in your arms---if you cut us we will bleed.

SKIDDING THROUGH LIFE

Walking down the road of some,
Singing the song of plenty,
Hoping for a miracle to come,
Knowing all alone – not any.
Nothing comes out of the blue,
To sit by your side and see,
Just how you are doing today and help you make your way.

You have to make the first step.
Some say the Bible always said,
And if you really believe than the Lord will make a way.

Don't you worry about those high bills?
Or how you can climb your debts hills.
Close your eyes and proclaim it loud,
You will make a way.

Have faith, my friend, and hold yourself still,
There is hope in everyday to get you up your hill.

LOVE

Love is like a newborn rose,
From its' stem it blooms and grows.
But if picked, it withers away;
Leaving nothing but a memory to stay.

HOPING AND THINKING

How many times have I wished upon a star?
So many times when my mind goes afar,
I wish I was in Hong Kong, I wish I was in Spain.
Oh, by wishing, things don't seem the same.

My mind goes to wondering and my head goes to ponder.
My body is still and reality is just a pretend memory.
But oh, how it hurts when there's a knock on the door,
And reality is here again; there is dreamland no more.

FAREWELL, MY BROTHER

Though we are still walking through the shadows of life,
And carrying the burden of just living,
We shall not forget you, dear brother, in
all our trials and misgivings.
We love you dearly, dear brother, you're always in our heart,
So rest for now until we see each other again,
And may the Lord bless you and rock
you sweetly within his bosom.

WE THE PEOPLE, PLANTS AND ANIMALS

And the Lord, God went into the mountain,
And after long hours of waiting for his return, he appeared.
As he descended from the mountain's path,
His face looked white as the fallen snow.

And the Lord, God fell upon his knees before us and prayed.
Today, we shall all rejoice in the prayers of our father,
And suffer each second in his grace and mercy.

MOTHER'S POEM

(Written and Dedicated to Michael's mother)

Thank you, Mother for making me the person I am
Thank you, for teaching me to be strong,
And how to stand in life alone.
Thank you, for teaching me to be wise,
And how to be weak and not to cry.
Thank you, for teaching me to think fast,
And how to solve life's problems as well as laugh.
Thank you, for teaching me to have consideration and patience,
And meditate upon my thoughts before I speak,
And how to pause and pray to thank my creator for this day.
Thank you, for teaching me to be honest and true,
And to learn through the years how to love you.
Thank you, for allowing me to walk many miles in your shoes,
Even though I am now full-grown and not living at home with you.
I smile even though I sometimes fight pain,
And appreciate the life you gave to me to persist and gain.
Thank you mother with all my heart,
For each lesson of life you taught.
I now live each day with love and nowadays I'm free,
Spreading your mother's wisdom and faith you gave me.
Thank you dear, mother.
I live my life each day as a mature man,
That follows his dreams and keeps his stand.

UNBALANCED

Sometimes my life seems to be trapped up in a haze,
And I get lost in its ever-changing maze.
The rain and fog from this darkness comes falling down,
Spreading its essence on me as I walk around with a frown.
I can't put this feeling into words so people can see,
So they can understand what's ailing me.
I don't want to give the impression that I am a fool,
But I rather people think that I am being cool.
Still I need to appear fragile and stout,
As I try to figure my life's problems out.
Ever shifting and continually heart-rending this haze of mine,
But that is called living, footsteps and lines.

MY NAME IS TROUBLE

How do I describe you and let people know,
You were my friend, protector and foe.
We had arguments, disagreements, hollering and funny words,
Still we made up and disagreements turned back to love.
You with your bag of potato chips and I with my pop,
Watched our favorite television programs
after we figured things out.
I miss you, old friend so very much,
But I remember your bark and your tail's touch.
Sometimes I still yell out "get off the sofa
or don't eat my leather shoe",
And remember that you would do what you wanted to do.
Now you are gone and I miss those days,
When you and I walked, ate, played and talked in phrase.
No one prepared me for you going home,
To dog's heaven and leaving me alone.
Sleep my loving furry friend,
Until you and I are united again.

JUST RATIONAL

I am here and I will stay,
I just want to run and play.
Enjoy the sun and dance in the rain,
Laugh and be happy without any pain.
Moods such as crying and self-reasoning within my mind,
Should take a vacation and stay a long time.
This would allow me to be happy without being sad,
Smile, sparkle and display to others how to be glad.
We are alive and here to stay,
Until it's time for us to die on that appointed day.
So enjoy and live a long life,
Living is delightful but then life offers strife.

FEATHER PLUCKED

What's wrong with me, I cannot say,
All I know is I cannot stay.
I am here just for this day,
But I will be gone soon by flying far away.
As high as I float within the wind and hide in the clouds,
I will not hear you shout or call out loud.
Then you will need to go it alone,
Don't look for me to come back home.

THE WAY

I have tried prayers and songs,
I have cried, yelled, begged and moaned.
I don't know anymore "what to do".
Hence now I'll just stop and wait on you.

So God please, tell me how to get to your house.
Tell me what fork in this road to take.
Tell me how my life will be.
Please Lord, for my soul's sake.
The more I try the more I seem to fail.
I need you Lord, I need you now.
I need to feel you presence within.
I need to know you're guiding my way.
I need to feel your arms around me.
And your spirit guiding me today.
God, please tell me how to get to your house.
Please don't send me the wrong way.
Tell me what direction on this road.
You deem my soul to take.

TIRED

I am tired and weary,
Life for me seems very dreary.
Please energize my soul.

No matter what I try to do,
I just can't seem to see it through.
Energize my soul.

My world appears to be crumbling down,
I walk in a daze wearing a frown.
Energize my soul.

When this old body is laid to rest,
Please Lord, let me feel my best.
Energize my soul.

LOOK AT ME

The wind danced as the water of the rain splashed upon the earth,
The trees moved to the motion of the wind and their leaves danced,
The mountains trembled as the lightning
clapped and thunder roared.
And the grass hollered, "keep pouring, we need more".
Quietness covered the earth as all waited without stirring to find,
What has happened to make the elements so unkind?
Sometimes a good cleaning is in order for all,
No matter how small, large or tall.
A fresh new start is what was needed.
Even though many did not understand and pleased.
He sat by the button and without a doubt.
Cleaned the world so all dwellers could have a new start.

UNANSWERED

I know,
I don't remember the answer,
I search,
I can't find where I placed it.
Looking through life items is like playing "hide and seek".
I try to guess where it is,
Mistaken places and no clues to where to look.
Forget this searching, I am tired.
Then one day, here is what I lost – right in front my face.

LIFE STINKS

Out of the depth of my fears,
Smelling bad and creeping near.
I hate my life and its turnabouts,
I despise the way events have turned out.
Pains and aches fill my days and nights,
Worries and fear of falling down,
Trying to keep up with others is turning me around.
Keeping up with others is hard to do,
Yet I still try very hard to.
Get you own life in check,
And quit mimicking others with your little speck.
Be proud of what you have and grin.
So pains and problems will not make you sin.

GAMES

Up the steps, down the steps, one by one,
Climb the ladder, symbolize that you have won.
Down the trees across the ditch,
Call ugly names symbolized you a witch.
Through the water, up the grass,
Can land you on sticks.
Life is wild and also tame,
Filled with plenty of woe and shame.
One by one there we go,
Taking on problems and asking for more.
Happy and sadness go hand in hand,
Playing out our daily role in life's games.

UNKNOWN

(Created for and dedicated to a friend)

Oh, please somebody hear my pledge,
I am alone out here on a ledge.
No matter whether I chose wrong or right,
I still seem to fight daily my pains and strive.
Sometimes I believe and other days I doubt,
I pray and beg for help to sort problems out.
I'm lost and found all at the same time,
I believe "I am crazy" and losing my mind.
No matter how loud I scream at you,
I still feel you will see me through.
Stress, joy, pain and doubt,
Just seems to seek me out.
Failure, losses and worry lasts days,
Smiles, good-feelings and love come in phases.
But today I am asking for help,
To quit hiding in this ball of kelp.

A SIMPLE PRAYER

Father, I have tried my way and failed.
I need your help in getting out of my jail.
I feel that you will bail me out,
Even if I have a million doubts.
I am asking with all my heart and soul,
Please, dear father, rewrite my scroll.
Let me enjoy my days on your earth,
Before my body is placed in your dirt.
I will keep my promise, you see,
Because this private hell is not for me.

IMAGINE ME

If I can imagine living in space,
Floating without gravity moving at a fast pace.
No need for cars, buses or trains,
Just me in my space suit and carrying my cane.

I can visit any planet I choose,
And stay as long as I am in the mood.
I can float pass a comet and wave goodbye,
I am the new space person and I can fly.

Wave at the sun
And mark the stars,
Fill my pocket with moon dust,
And blow it toward Mars.

Live my life with profound bliss,
Give out many space hugs with a kiss.
Oh, what a beautiful life this will be,
Mimicking all the animals that live in the sea.

WHISPERS

Come here let me tell you something I just heard,
But you can't tell others, they will think it's absurd.
Let me put in your ear so no one will know,
This gossip I learned about a banjo.
Pluck its strings and hear a tune,
Tap your feet and dance under the moon.
Don't share this gossip with anyone else, Or
you will pay for what you said yourself.

RAIN

Watery droplets upon my shirt,
Dancing around my stain of dirt.
Millions of drops falling on me,
Chasing my clothes not allowing the dryness to be.
Conquering the dryness of everything I have on,
As well as wetting my purse and my phone.

Falling from the sky without a care,
Filling the earth's landscape as if giving it a dare.
Who will stop my droplets from falling?
Any and every place I choose them to be?
Because you are my captive, and my water is free.
Wait until I go home,
Then everything can dry out and you can sing me a song.

THEY

One by one the people came,
No one bothered to ask their name.
Except for one, they were all the same,
Walking through the door of shame.
One by one, two by two, three by three and four by four,
All the people came through the one door.
Only two words were used to describe them all – THEY CAME.

BROKE

I'm just sitting here thinking about my plight,
I know I should do something to ease my pain.

Instead I just sit here allowing the shame,
I know thinking about this can't end my blight,
But still, I have no courage to start to fight.

The night is long and dark without light,
I ain't got a nickel or any money in sight,
The pain is deeper as the hours pass.

I can't stop the minutes that pass to make amends,
I hope and wish the end to my problem in sight,
But I know just worrying can't change a thing.

I just feel sorry for the shape I'm in,
Maybe tomorrow's thing will be better in a way,
But for now this is all I can say.

I ain't got a nickel or any money in sight,
I got to hold on and don't give up the fight,
I'm just sitting here thinking about my plight.

STROLL

I've walked the world with the dinosaurs and saw all there is to see,
I've talked to the flying doves and learned
what man will need to be.
I've climbed the majestic mountain tops,
And spoke to the winds at sea,
I've never wondered how or why that God made things to be.
With all my travels to the four corners
of earth, and the sights to see,
I still kneel on my knees and give thanks to thee.
You provided the lights to wondering souls
and keep the world amaze,
You clear minds and open the eyes to see your celestial ways.
You help when no one else cares; never thinking we are fools,
You dear God have granted us life but still
some of us don't think it's cool.

NOT ME

Who never yells at you or curses at you but only whispers softly in your ear?
Who loves us endlessly and gives to us tenderness and choices?
Who never begs you to make a choice but only waits patiently for your decision?
Who knows all our secrets yet never tells anyone?

Who never complains to you about your weight but only carries you when you can't walk another step?
Who never tells you how ugly you look but only accepts you as the beautiful goddess you are?

Who lingers at your bedside night and day during sickness and good health but stays close to you at all times to protect you from all your good times and bad hurts?
Who allows you to wipe the sweat from your brows as you create your footsteps of living?

Who holds your hand and guides you through your hurts; comforts you when you fall from grace; hold you when you grieve through the thorns of death and carries you when times are hard and hopeless, but never charges, or place hidden fees upon your soul?

Who walks trillions of miles with you to keep your steps steady without criticizing who you are? Who can we count on any hour of the day or night for help; or help us find answers when we can't think because we are lost? Who is there when everyone else has gone home? God is our shepherd; our everlasting father.

SHORT STORIES

THE PARTING OF BROTHERS

"We-e-e, look at me!" the moon sang across the sky. "No, no, look at me", the sun bellowed for all to hear. "I can bounce on the clouds higher than the moon", he roared. The sun and the moon often played together on the billowy, puffy clouds. "Just look at them out here occupying the sky at the same time", the giant cloud named Angus huffed. They're jumping all over our backs. They know that both of them can't be outside at the same time", Lil Pearl cloud stated. "One of us clouds should make one of them go inside", he added.

Silver Moon was busy playing, but not so busy he couldn't hear his friends, the clouds. He became very angry at what they were saying about him and his brother. "How can you, Angus, say such a thing," he questioned. "You know very well I can move through the sky anytime I want to and no one can make me go inside. I can make you go in," Sun Shine boasted with a big shiny smile on his face. "I can make you go inside anytime I want you to leave", he added.

"You can't do a thing, Sun Shine, dear brother," Silver Moon anxiously replied. "Well now," Sun Shine echoed, "that sounds like a challenge to me. I like a good challenge, especially from you, Silver Moon". "Well, Silver Moon added, let the game start now."

Silver Moon rapidly moved to the south corner of the sky. Smiling very devilish, Sun Shine moved to the west section of the sky. Angus and Lil Pearl cloud hovered amid the two giants, waiting to see who would make the first move. "Angus", Lil Pearl whispered, "we should have been more careful in speaking out loud about them two. You know how sensitive those two brothers can get". "You're right", Angus muttered in reply. "We both know that those two can fight for days without anyone giving in. Just watch yourself, Lil Pearl", Angus added firmly. "Maybe we can find a way to stop this challenge".

Sun Shine began to shine his majestic, magical rays down on the earth. Shades of yellow, blue, orange, green and gold danced past the clouds and entangled themselves as they fell upon the earth. Silver

Moon beamed his silvery reflection just as Sun Shine rays reached the earth, too. "Look at him", Silver Moon yelled disgustedly loud. "How his rays make me angry". "Come, Twinkle Stars and gather around me to add more sparkle to my glowing", he commanded. Twinkle Stars moved their cluster over to their friend, Silver Moon side of the sky. Together with his reflection, they added a bright and sassy sparkle to his shimmer.

Sun Shine looked jealously upon his brother's reflection and bellowed loudly to his friends. "Why can't someone adorn my lovely rays and make them even finer?" he pleaded. Angus and Lil Pearl cloud quickly moved over to help him. But their action only caused a problem for Sun Shine. You see, as Angus and Lil Pearl cloud tried to shine with the sun, they only blocked his rays and this allowed Silver Moon's reflection to look more beautiful upon the earth.

Sun Shine became angrier as the minutes passed by. The more he tried to beat Silver Moon's beautiful reflections, the harder and hotter his rays shone upon the earth. Steam began to rise like a large misty cloud from the earths' core to the sky, as his rays became hotter and hotter.

Arriving on the scene from visiting his friends in the east, the North Wind made a swift decision. Seeing what was happening in his sky and on his earth, he immediately went to work. Gathering all his strength, he let out a tremendous blow of air and knocked Silver Moon and Twinkle Stars into another dimension called NIGHT. As he turned his winds on Sun Shine to blow him away, Sun Shine hollered to him with a sharp, urgent cry. "Wait", he cried, "I am not angry anymore. The game is over. If you would allow me to shine now, old mighty wind, I will call this time DAY. I promise I will shine for a short time each day and then allow my brother, Silver Moon, to show the earth his reflection called NIGHT".

North Wind thought very carefully about the promise Sun Shine was making. "We will try your way, old mighty sun", he roared through the sky. "But if the moon starts to disagree with you again, I will not be so kind".

Silver Moon smiled along with his friends, Twinkle Stars. They liked their new home called Night and they were glad that Sun Shine had made such a promise to North Wind. They did not want to share the sky with him anymore.

Now the SUN rules the DAY and the MOON and STARS rules the NIGHT.

The NORTH WINDS rules both NIGHT and DAY as a reminder to both brothers to keep the peace upon the earth.

Moral: Separation can be for the better sometimes.

JOHNNY NECKTIE

Johnny Necktie yearned for the day he would be placed around his owner's shirt collar and gently caress his neck muscles. He often dreamed of adding sparkle to his owner's dress suits. But to his dismay, time passed and still he just hung around his owner's clothes closet, clinging loosely on a hook that was embedded into the wall.

Each morning Johnny Necktie put on his best designer face as his owner quickly opened the closet door, chose, and hurriedly closed the door behind him.

Johnny Necktie never gave up hope until he heard the front door slam as his owner raced to his car. Suddenly, Johnny Necktie became sad. Since he arrived at his new home, not a day or night was he selected to be worn with any of his owner's suits? He came in a well-fashioned tie box and as he remembered his owner was very happy to get him. For a long time his owner just stared at him in his black and gold box with a small green bowtie ribbon on it. Johnny Necktie was very excited when he first came to live in his new house. Now even his beloved box was gone and replaced with an old brown weathered hook he called home.

Johnny Necktie wondered why his owner hadn't chosen him since he came to him one year ago. After all, he was made from the best silk material money could buy and he carried a very expensive price tag. Still, Johnny Necktie was not good enough for his owner's suits. The lady who brought him from his home at the store had chosen him from all the other ties on his long rack and surprised his new owner with him as a gift. All the other ties in his owner's closet were daintily placed on a glass and brass neck tie holder while Johnny Necktie lay across on an old rusty hook pounded into the closet wall. Each tie hung in a wrinkle-free position in full view of all the suits in the closet. They even had their own spacing built into the rack. "What a fine life they are having", Johnny Necktie thought.

But he had one thing all the other ties did not possess. You see

Johnny Necktie had colors. His material exploded with very unique colors. His soft silk gusted with the yellow and gold woven with a hint of black traced in a geometrical pattern on its front. Johnny Necktie could not understand why his owner opted to always wear his plain cotton blue, dark blue, black, midnight black, brown, dark brown, tan, beige, dark beige, soft beige and pale white ties but did not select his brilliant hues to add luster to his equally plain suits.

Time passed slowly and Johnny Necktie soon stopped trying to get his owner's attention when the closet door opened. Instead of trying he just dropped his body and swayed to the air that came into the closet when the door opened and closed. He had succumbed to being lost in the closet world forever. He had great hopes of making his owner's appearance very fashionable when he came to live in his new home but now he just wished to find a nice spot on the closet floor away from his owner's footsteps. These days he only wanted to fall carelessly into a remote spot, preferable, under his owner's old long winter coat that hung down onto the floor and hide for the rest of his life. No one would miss him, he thought, because no one ever moved that old coat. "How can I add glamour to that coat?", he often thought to himself. "He and I would make a very good team. His brown fur would complement my colors exceptionally. But now never will the sun shine upon my silk material face or people gaze at my lovely design," he sighed. The more the closet door opened, the closer Johnny Necktie drooped toward the closet floor.

The old worn hook did nothing to save him from dropping off of its back. "He just has to learn to live with his fate," the old hook reasoned.

Sometimes to pass time, Johnny Necktie allowed himself to remember his days at the department store with his other tie brothers. He often thought about the fun they had playing whose going to buy me next. No one felt left out of the game and everyone shared a sense of happiness for the winners of the day. But when the reality of his new existence filled his material he became sad. Johnny Necktie had lost hope within his fabric.

One day the closet door opened and his owner stepped in. Instead of his arms and hands reaching straight toward the closet tie holder, he ran his fingers nervously along the clothes rack as if he was looking for something. Johnny Necktie didn't look up. He was so close to the closet floor and his new hiding place that he could see it. Suddenly, he felt a pant leg brushed again his colorful fabric. "Oh my, I've been looking for you," his owner surprisingly said. "We are supposed to wear something colorful and stylish to the office today and I'm going to wear you", he added. "I really forgot where I had placed you. I was hoping I didn't throw you away. I don't wear ties like your kind but a request is a request. I don't think putting you on this one time would hurt. I don't want to be the only one without color today," he chatted as he dressed.

Johnny Necktie could not believe what he was hearing. He did not move a thread. Suddenly, Johnny Necktie felt joy as his gentle fabric was placed around his owner's neck and a brand new brown dress shirt collar flipped nicely over his middle. He delicately allowed his full silk material to be dropped upon his owner's chest. "Well, we will see how this goes over today," his owner nervously said as he opened the door.

One last look in the hall mirror and out the door Johnny Necktie and his owner went. "Hey, nice tie," his owners neighbor called out to him. "Where did you get it because I want one?" "You want this old tie," his owner replied. "Sure I do," his neighbor answered. "If it makes you and your suit look good that is definitely a tie I need. It makes you look very different and man, you really needed a change," he added. His owner smiled. "That's a nice tie, Sir," the lady at the stop sign hollered. "That tie makes your suit look good." His owner laughed as he turned the corner heading for work.

"Gosh, you look good in that suit and tie", his secretary said as she looked him up and down. "That tie really does add to your appearance", she added. "It's good to see you add some color to your wardrobe." Johnny Necktie's owner received compliments the entire day about his choice of tie. He was very happy. He never thought a colorful tie would cause him to add a touch of sparkle to his everyday appearance. He promised himself that Johnny Necktie would never be placed on that weathered hook again and he would have other colorful ties for his company. He also promised Johnny Necktie that he would wear him often with his suits. Johnny Necktie was very happy and his silky fabric sparkled.

Moral: When life colors your world the darkest hue, never give up hope.

THOMAS, THE BOTTLE

Long ago in a place called Ocean; there lived a bottle name Thomas Bottlehead. Thomas was a very smooth, tall and lean water bottle that lived on the sands in Ocean Place. The sand was friends to a long stretch of water that lived in Ocean. Sometimes, especially when the winds of Ocean blew fast, the water would decide to send its watery waves to cover the sand. The waves would move back and forth over the sand and then return home. The sands loved how the watery waves scratched their bodies and removed all the small itches it had collected.

Thomas loved his home. When the wind blew, he would roll up and down the sand. He would allow the breeze to blow through his bottle cap and clean his inside. Sometimes he would get stuck in the sand's holes, but small critters that made their home in the sand would push him out. He loved to sleep under the moon and starry sky, and awake with the sun's rays. He was happy but he wanted to find others of his kind.

One day as Thomas rolled in the wind; his bottle cap dug itself in the sand and his bottle stopped suddenly to watch a gigantic wave of water flowing back and forth over the sand miles away from his path. He was truly surprised. "Where is that watery thing going?", he shouted to the small critters that were gathering food nearby. "Aren't you afraid of that thing?" The critters laughed and went about their busy day. Thomas could only stare at the water.

He remembered how one-time the water fell from the sun and splashed sand everywhere including within his body. The water did not visit the sand very long but still he remembered that day. Later that watery day, the sand that stained the inside of his body, jumped out of his body with the help of liquid. He felt free from the heavy weight of the sand and the sun's rays shone through his body again.

"There must be something magical about this wet stuff," Thomas reasoned to himself. "After all, there would not be so much of it in Ocean, if it was not magical".

For several days, Thomas would roll himself to the place he saw the giant waves of water. He would lie on the sand and dream about the day he found the wave. Time passed as Thomas waited to see the wave again. By chance, as he was visiting the spot, a colossal wave of water fell upon the sand. Thomas could not roll fast enough to safety so the wave picked him up and pressed him into its bosom as it nestled him in its magical liquid. He could not move.

Thomas was afraid. He opened his bottle cap half-way to release the tension of his bottle. Then some of the magical liquid raced into his body. He flipped upright as the liquid bounced up and down within him. As he bounced, another smaller wave grasped him and lifted him high into the sky. This motion went on for several minutes, as Thomas fought very hard to relax. He wished he was back on the sands rolling lazily in the sun. He let out a sigh and decided he would accept his fate in the liquid.

Thomas looked out from the water's grasp and saw the sand he loved so fondly very far away from him. He realized he was now surrounded in a massive pool of magical liquid. The magical waves moved and danced with his body. His body moved and danced with the magical liquid waves. The liquid stroked his body and caressed his cap as it seemed to rock him very lovingly as he moved with its ripples. Thomas felt how the liquid covered his body for a few seconds and then it would float with its current. He liked what was happening to him.

He bobbed up and down and twisted over the waves. To his surprise, a school of dolphins took him by his bottle cap and played water tag with him. When they left him, Thomas bounced on the sharks back and chased the sea turtles as they swan home. Thomas never thought he could have so much fun in this magical liquid.

He loved to play games in the water that lived by the sand. He made new friends and Otis, the octopus wrapped his long arms around his body, lifted his cap and filled his body with the magical liquid and placed the cap back. "This way", he told Thomas, "you can come to visit whenever you wish to". Then Otis threw him back to the sands. Otis told him when he wanted to play in the liquid, just roll to the waves and come and play.

With his bottle filled with the magical liquid, Thomas rolled and laughed as he moved over the sand to find a place to rest. He was happy. After that day, he never worried about finding others because he had many, many friends in the magical liquid.

GOODBYE

I won't go,
But I must.
I can't go.
But I will.
I don't want to say goodbye,
But I can't overstay my welcome.

Thank you for reading my words.

As you add your footsteps, you are not alone.
Some of us share the moods and phrases that are assigned to each of
us when we are born. Take care!!

Pattie

Printed in the United States
By Bookmasters